Growing Older Gracefully: Embracing aging with Purpose and J

I am an eighty-seven-year-old widow, blessed with seven living children, though I've also known the deep pain of losing two. My life has been one of many seasons, each guided by a sense of purpose. As a mother and wife, I was able to return to school, first earning my high school diploma, then a Bachelor's in Social Work (BSW), and later a Master's in Social Work (MSW). Even now, I continue to learn because I believe learning is the key to living a life of purpose, no matter your age.

I want to express my inspiration for writing this book. My mother Inez Stephens was one of the most amazing women I ever met. She never received a high school diploma but was a very educated woman. My mother was always learning something new. She was a stay-at home mother, but she sewed for many of the wealthy people in the community. She made flowers, taught music and made hats. My mother had a dedicated husband who always called her his 'doll.' My mother at ninety-two was still able to sit on the floor because she was always 'hemming in' someone's dress or a man's pants.

My mother was a stylish woman who still wore high heeled shoes at ninety-two years old. I know I got my sense of style from her, but it wasn't always that way. She was a woman of great wisdom and was always taking care of other people, she was a woman of prayer who many times prayed all night. As my mother aged, we connected and became great friends. I will share more about her through the eyes of my niece who wrote about her grandmother in the following pages.

There were times when balancing family, work, and studies felt overwhelming, but it was during those moments that I discovered how strong a sense of purpose can be. It kept me moving forward, even when it seemed easier to give up. Those experiences taught me that our purpose evolves as we do, and it is never too late to grow into who we are meant to be. This book is not just about growing older; it's about growing wiser, deeper, and more fulfilled. It is my hope that these pages will inspire you—whether you are young and unsure of your direction, or older and feeling that your time for dreaming has passed—to reflect on your own purpose. If we still have breath in our lungs, we still have a purpose to fulfill.

Inez Mitchell Riddick Stephens – Tribute written by her granddaughter (my niece, Robin Riddick).

"My earliest memory was of her, my momma and myself riding in a car, headed to the shops. I'm not sure of whom the car belonged to, but she drove it like it was hers. Our main objective was to purchase back-to-school clothes for my siblings and me. Strange memory, right? It was raining and evening-time-dark. I remember the headlights of other cars as they passed by us. My grandma Inez (designated driver) and my momma were chattering back and forth up front.

(Side Note here: Through the many years they spent as mother and daughter-in-law, they would remain the best of friends.)

Back to the story: And from what I could understand about driving, as a youth, it seemed that neither of them were really concentrating on the road, traffic patterns, or traffic lights. Their conversation ranged from one subject to another, wherein, I couldn't grasp the meaning behind any of it. Although, at one point, I did hear my grandmother ask my momma, "What do the children need for school?" Immediately, my mom responded with, "Underwear". She told everyone, it seemed to me, that the perfect gifts for her kids were something we couldn't play with or eat. Disgusted, I went back to my childish thoughts.

Even 25 years after her death, this memory is alive in my head. My grandma COULD DRIVE! Back then I am sure not many women drove or probably owned a car. But my amazing grandmother did. I also witnessed her BE GREAT at anything else she touched. She was the best seamstress this side of the Mississippi. She made hats, dresses, and invited everyone to her fashion shows, which were mainly held in her home. She also dabbled in upholstery, and draperies with swags and such. Her love for the piano became a passion to such a degree that she yearned to teach others her skills __ her gift! I even attempted to harness her knack for playing and use it for my gain. Alas, it would not be so! While her fingers flowed over the ivory and ebony keys, mine would not!

Time spent with her outside of duties was precious in my sight. She traveled with my parents and my siblings on many occasions. She was there in the back seat of my daddy's Oldsmobile, as we drove from Virginia to California to visit my oldest sister, her husband and baby boy, and my brother who had been stationed at a Naval base there. It took us five days to get there. And five days on the return trip. My goodness! What an adventure! Priceless in my sight! Laughter and good conversation mingled with plenty of naps.

Wisdom words sprang from her mouth every time she opened it. And I clung to each one. I miss her in every way possible. The situations that I find myself in these days, she would have an answer to, I am sure! She found them in Jesus the Christ. Rooted in Scripture, and like a tree planted by the water, nothing could convince her to step outside of God. I was privileged to walk alongside her, while she journeyed through the earth. Like Ruth, I gleaned as much as I could, which led to wholeness in my life! Thank you, Grandma Inez!"

Defining *Growing Older Gracefully*:
1. **Embracing Aging with Acceptance**: This means acknowledging the changes that come with age—physical, emotional, and social—without resisting them. Instead of focusing on trying to remain youthful, one embraces their age with dignity and self-compassion.
2. **Maintaining Physical and Mental Health**: For some, growing older gracefully means making efforts to stay physically active and mentally sharp. This includes eating healthy,

exercising, and engaging in activities that challenge the mind, such as learning new skills or hobbies.

3. **Cultivating Emotional and Spiritual Well-being**: This perspective involves focusing on personal growth, emotional balance, and spiritual fulfillment. It could mean deepening one's relationship with God, finding peace in one's faith, or fostering inner calm and resilience.

4. **Remaining Engaged with Life**: People who age gracefully often stay connected to the world around them—whether through family, community, work, or hobbies. They remain curious and involved, refusing to let age limit their participation in life.

5. **Embracing Inner Beauty and Wisdom**: Rather than prioritizing external appearances, this approach values the wisdom and depth that come with age. It's about cultivating kindness, patience, and understanding, knowing that these traits reflect inner beauty more than superficial youth.

6. **Letting Go of Perfection**: Growing older gracefully also means relinquishing the pursuit of perfection and accepting imperfections—whether they are wrinkles, physical limitations, or the loss of certain abilities. It's about finding peace in imperfection.

7. **Living with Gratitude and Purpose**: Many see graceful aging as living with gratitude for each day and continuing to pursue a purpose, whether it's through helping others, mentoring, or contributing to the community.

Each person's definition can reflect their personal values, cultural influences, and life journey.

Introduction

Aging is a natural part of life's journey, a process that brings with it a unique blend of challenges and opportunities. For many, the prospect of growing older can be daunting, filled with concerns about health, independence, and purpose. However, aging also offers a profound chance for growth, self-discovery, and renewal. This book, **"Growing Older Gracefully: Embracing Aging with Purpose and Joy,"** is an invitation to explore the possibilities of aging with intention and joy, to redefine what it means to grow older, and to live each day with purpose and vitality.

In today's society, there are many misconceptions and fears surrounding aging. We often hear negative narratives that focus on decline, loss, and limitation. Yet, this perspective overlooks the richness, wisdom, and strength that comes with age. Aging gracefully is not about resisting the passage of time or clinging to youth; it's about embracing the fullness of life, cultivating resilience, and finding meaning in every stage of our lives.

This book is designed to guide you through the journey of aging with grace, empowering you to take charge of your well-being and cultivate a positive mindset that fosters growth and renewal. We will explore the powerful role of mindset in shaping our experiences of aging, how self-acceptance can transform our relationship with ourselves, and the importance of self-care in nurturing our physical, emotional, and spiritual health.

You will find practical strategies and insights to help you:

- **Challenge Common Misconceptions and Fears About Aging:** Understand the myths that surround aging and replace them with a more empowering, life-affirming perspective.
- **Embrace Self-Acceptance and the Aging Process:** Learn to love and accept yourself at every stage, embracing your life story with compassion and grace. • **Harness the Power of Mindset:** Discover how a positive, growth-oriented mindset can transform your experience of aging, enabling you to live with purpose, joy, and resilience.
- **Prioritize Self-Care and Wellness:** Explore the vital importance of caring for your mind, body, and spirit, and find practical tips to enhance your well-being.

Aging is not merely about getting older; it is about evolving, adapting, and continuing to grow. It is about recognizing the beauty of each season of life and making the most of the years we have. This book is your companion in this journey, offering wisdom, encouragement, and practical advice to help you navigate the path ahead with confidence and grace.

Whether you are just beginning to think about aging or are well into your later years, this book will provide valuable insights and tools to help you live fully and joyfully. It's time to redefine aging, not as a period of decline but as a time of renewal, growth, and profound possibility. Let's embark on this journey together, embracing each moment with an open heart and a spirit of adventure.

Chapter 1. Common Misconceptions and Fears About Aging

Aging is a universal experience, yet it is often misunderstood and surrounded by myths and misconceptions. These misunderstandings can create unnecessary fears and anxieties, preventing us from embracing the aging process with grace and positivity. Let's explore some of the most common misconceptions and fears about aging and how we can challenge them.

1. Misconception: Aging Means Becoming Irrelevant or Useless

One of the most pervasive myths about aging is that older adults become irrelevant, less valuable, or useless. This misconception is fueled by a culture that often prioritizes youth and novelty over experience and wisdom. The fear of becoming "obsolete" can lead to anxiety about aging and a reluctance to grow older.

Reality: Aging brings a wealth of experience, knowledge, and insight that is invaluable. Many older adults contribute significantly to their communities, families, and workplaces. Rather than becoming irrelevant, aging individuals often find new ways to engage and impact the world around them. Embracing this reality helps combat the fear of becoming useless and encourages a more positive outlook on aging.

2. Misconception: Aging Equals Decline and Disease

Another common misconception is that aging is synonymous with decline and illness. While it is true that the risk of certain health conditions increases with age, aging does not automatically mean a decline in quality of life or health.

Reality: Many older adults live vibrant, healthy lives well into their later years. With advances in medicine, nutrition, and fitness, it is possible to maintain a high level of physical and mental health as we age. Regular exercise, a balanced diet, and proactive healthcare can significantly reduce the risk of age-related diseases and promote longevity and well-being.

3. Misconception: Aging Leads to Loneliness and Isolation

The fear of becoming lonely and isolated is another significant concern for many people as they age. This fear is often based on the assumption that older adults are more likely to lose social connections due to retirement, the death of loved ones, or mobility limitations. **Reality:** While social dynamics may change with age, many older adults remain socially active and engaged. Community groups, faith organizations, volunteer opportunities, and technology can help older adults maintain and even expand their social networks. Developing new friendships and staying connected with family and friends are crucial for emotional well-being, regardless of age.

4. Misconception: Cognitive Decline is Inevitable

Many people fear that aging will lead to inevitable cognitive decline or dementia. This fear is heightened by media portrayals that often associate aging with forgetfulness or confusion.

Reality: While some cognitive changes are normal as we age, severe cognitive decline is not a guaranteed part of aging. Many older adults maintain sharp cognitive functions throughout their lives. Engaging in mental activities such as reading, puzzles, learning new skills, and social interaction can help keep the mind sharp. Moreover, a healthy lifestyle that includes physical activity, a nutritious diet, and good sleep can significantly support cognitive health.

5. Misconception: Aging Means Losing Independence

The fear of losing independence is a common concern among older adults. This fear often stems from the idea that aging automatically results in a loss of physical or mental abilities, making individuals dependent on others.

Reality: While some older adults may require assistance due to health issues, many maintain their independence well into their later years. Advances in healthcare, adaptive technologies, and supportive community resources can help individuals maintain their independence. Planning for future needs, such as making home modifications or exploring community services, can empower older adults to live independently and comfortably.

6. Misconception: Aging is Something to Fear

Many people fear aging itself, associating it with negative stereotypes and the unknown. This fear can be exacerbated by societal attitudes and media portrayals that emphasize the challenges rather than the opportunities of aging.

Reality: Aging is a natural part of life and can be a time of growth, fulfillment, and new opportunities. It is a period when many people find deeper meaning, purpose, and connection. By shifting the focus from fear to acceptance and embracing the positive aspects of aging, individuals can experience a richer, more rewarding later life.

Overcoming Misconceptions and Fears

Understanding and challenging these common misconceptions and fears about aging is crucial for embracing the aging process with grace and positivity. Education, open conversations, and a shift in cultural attitudes can help dispel myths and reduce fears. By focusing on the opportunities for growth, learning, and connection that come with aging, we can foster a more positive and empowering perspective on growing older.

Chapter 2. Nurturing the Mind and Spirit

Aging gracefully is not just about maintaining physical health; it's also about nurturing the mind and spirit to foster a sense of fulfillment, joy, and purpose. As we grow older, investing in mental and spiritual well-being becomes even more crucial. This chapter explores practical strategies for keeping the mind sharp and the spirit strong, highlighting the importance of continuous learning, emotional resilience, spiritual growth, and mindfulness. This chapter will encourage you to embrace practices that bring clarity, peace and a deeper sense of connection. It will help you navigate the aging process with grace and fulfillment.

The Power of Continuous Learning

- **Keeping the Mind Sharp**: Engaging in lifelong learning helps maintain cognitive function, enhances creativity, and keeps the mind agile. Research shows that learning new skills and challenging the brain can help delay cognitive decline and improve memory. Embrace activities that stimulate the brain, such as reading, puzzles, learning a new language, or taking up a musical instrument.
- **Practical Ways to Learn**: Consider taking courses online or at local community centers, joining book clubs or discussion groups, and exploring new hobbies. Learning isn't confined to formal education; it can also involve exploring interests and passions that keep the mind engaged and curious.
- **Cultivating a Growth Mindset**: Adopting a growth mindset, the belief that abilities and intelligence can be developed, encourages you to see aging as an opportunity for continued growth and discovery. This mindset fosters resilience, adaptability, and a positive outlook, making it easier to embrace new experiences and challenges.

Emotional Resilience and Well-being

- **Understanding Emotional Resilience**: Emotional resilience is the ability to cope with and recover from life's challenges. Developing emotional resilience helps you navigate the emotional ups and downs that can come with aging, such as dealing with loss, health changes, or retirement.
- **Building Emotional Resilience**: Practice self-compassion and mindfulness to stay grounded in the present moment. Develop healthy coping strategies, such as maintaining a strong social network, engaging in hobbies, and practicing gratitude. These practices help build a resilient mindset that can handle the stresses and uncertainties of aging.

- **The Role of Positive Relationships**: Relationships are crucial for emotional wellbeing. Maintaining and nurturing positive relationships with family, friends, and community members can provide emotional support and reduce feelings of isolation or loneliness. Actively seek out and cultivate connections that bring joy and meaning to your life.

Spiritual Growth and Purpose

- **Exploring Spirituality**: Spirituality can be a source of comfort, strength, and a sense of purpose. It often involves reflecting on life's bigger questions, finding meaning in experiences, and connecting with something greater than oneself. Spirituality isn't limited to religious practices; it can be found in nature, art, service to others, or meditation.
- **Practices for Spiritual Growth**: Engage in practices that nurture your spirit, such as prayer, meditation, yoga, or spiritual reading. These practices can help you feel more connected to yourself, others, and the world around you. They can also provide a sense of peace and acceptance, helping you navigate the aging process with grace.
- **Finding Purpose and Meaning**: As you age, finding a renewed sense of purpose can enhance your well-being and provide motivation. Reflect on what brings you joy, fulfillment, and a sense of contribution. This might involve volunteering, mentoring, pursuing creative passions, or engaging in community activities that align with your values.

Mindfulness and Meditation for Clarity and Peace

- **The Benefits of Mindfulness**: Mindfulness involves being fully present in the moment, cultivating awareness without judgment. Practicing mindfulness can reduce stress, improve focus, and enhance emotional regulation. It helps shift attention away from worries about the future or regrets about the past, fostering a sense of peace and acceptance.
- **Incorporating Mindfulness into Daily Life**: Simple mindfulness practices, such as mindful breathing, mindful walking, or body scanning, can be easily integrated into daily routines. These practices help cultivate a sense of calm and clarity, making it easier to navigate the challenges and changes that come with aging. • **Meditation for Mental and Emotional Health**: Regular meditation practice can enhance mental clarity, reduce anxiety, and promote emotional stability. Different types of meditation, such as guided meditation, loving-kindness meditation, or meditation on Bible verses, can be explored to find what resonates best with you. Even a few minutes of meditation each day can significantly impact your overall well-being.

Creating a Holistic Routine for Mind and Spirit

- **Developing a Balanced Daily Routine**: Establish a daily routine that incorporates activities to nurture both the mind and spirit. This could include starting the day with a few minutes of meditation or prayer, engaging in learning activities, taking time for reflection or journaling, and ending the day with gratitude practices.
- **Integrating Physical, Mental, and Spiritual Practices**: A holistic approach to aging involves integrating physical exercise with mental and spiritual practices. Activities

like walking and listening with mindfulness and meditation, offering benefits for both the body and mind. Similarly, walking in nature or gardening can provide physical exercise while also nurturing the spirit.

- **Finding Joy in Simple Practices**: Nurturing the mind and spirit doesn't have to be complex or time-consuming. Find joy in simple daily practices that bring peace, clarity, and connection. Whether it's reading a book, listening to music, spending time in nature, or practicing gratitude, these small acts can significantly impact your overall sense of well-being.

Embracing a Journey of Self-Discovery

- **Reflecting on Your Journey**: Aging is an opportunity to reflect on your life's journey, recognizing your growth, achievements, and the wisdom gained along the way. Embrace this period as a time of self-discovery, where you can explore new interests, deepen your spirituality, and connect more deeply with yourself and others.
- **Continuing to Grow and Evolve**: Understand that nurturing the mind and spirit is a lifelong journey that evolves. Remain open to new experiences, learning opportunities, and spiritual insights. By continuously nurturing your mind and spirit, you can approach aging with a sense of curiosity, resilience, and joy.

Remember, a nurturing mind and spirit is essential for aging gracefully with purpose and joy. By engaging in continuous learning, cultivating emotional resilience, nurturing spiritual growth, and practicing mindfulness, you can enhance your mental and spiritual well-being.

The Power of Mindset in Aging Gracefully

Mindset is a powerful tool that shapes how we perceive and experience the world. As we age, our mindset plays a crucial role in determining how we navigate the physical, emotional, and social changes that come with growing older. A positive, growth-oriented mindset can significantly enhance our ability to age gracefully, fostering resilience, wellbeing, and a sense of purpose.

1. Understanding Mindset

Mindset refers to the beliefs and attitudes we hold about ourselves and the world around us. Psychologist Carol Dweck introduced the concepts of "fixed mindset" and "growth mindset" to describe how individuals approach challenges and opportunities:

- **Fixed Mindset:** Believing that our abilities, intelligence, and traits are static and unchangeable. With a fixed mindset, people may see aging as a period of inevitable decline and limitation.
- **Growth Mindset:** Believing that our abilities and intelligence can develop through effort, learning, and perseverance. With a growth mindset, aging is viewed as an opportunity for continued growth, learning, and adaptation.

Adopting a growth mindset can transform our experience of aging, allowing us to embrace change, learn new skills, and maintain a positive outlook on life.

2. The Impact of Mindset on Physical Health

Research has shown that our mindset can have a profound impact on our physical health as we age. Individuals with a positive outlook on aging are more likely to engage in healthy behaviors, such as regular exercise, balanced nutrition, and routine medical check-ups. They are also more likely to recover from illness or injury and experience fewer chronic conditions.

The Role of a Positive Mindset: A positive mindset can help reduce stress, boost the immune system, and promote healthy aging. By believing that we have control over our health and well-being, we are more likely to take proactive steps to maintain our physical fitness and manage health challenges effectively.

3. Mindset and Emotional Well-Being

Our mindset also affects our emotional well-being as we age. A positive mindset can foster resilience, allowing us to cope more effectively with the emotional challenges that come with aging, such as loss, grief, or changes in social roles.

The Power of Optimism: An optimistic mindset encourages us to focus on the positive aspects of life, find meaning in our experiences, and maintain a sense of purpose. This outlook can enhance our emotional resilience, helping us to navigate the ups and downs of aging with grace and confidence. **4. Mindset and Cognitive Health**

There is a strong link between mindset and cognitive health. A growth mindset encourages continuous learning and mental stimulation, which are critical for maintaining cognitive function as we age. Engaging in activities that challenge the brain—such as puzzles, reading, learning new skills, or social interaction—can help keep the mind sharp and reduce the risk of cognitive decline.

Embracing Lifelong Learning: By maintaining a curious and open-minded approach to life, we can continue to grow intellectually and emotionally. This mindset fosters a love of learning and encourages us to explore new interests, hobbies, and skills, enriching our lives and enhancing cognitive vitality.

5. Shifting Negative Perceptions About Aging

Many people hold negative perceptions about aging, viewing it as a time of loss, decline, or irrelevance. These beliefs can become self-fulfilling prophecies, leading to decreased motivation, social withdrawal, and a decline in physical and mental health.

Reframing Aging as a Positive Experience: Shifting to a more positive mindset about aging involves reframing these perceptions. Instead of focusing on what is lost, we can focus on what is gained—wisdom, experience, freedom, and opportunities for growth. This shift in perspective can lead to a more fulfilling and meaningful experience of aging.

6. The Role of Gratitude in Aging Gracefully

Practicing gratitude is a powerful way to cultivate a positive mindset. By focusing on the blessings and opportunities that come with each stage of life, we can foster a sense of appreciation and contentment. Gratitude can enhance our overall sense of well-being and help us navigate the aging process with grace and positivity.

Gratitude Practice: Simple practices such as keeping a gratitude journal, reflecting on daily blessings, or expressing thanks to others can help cultivate a positive and appreciative mindset. This focus on gratitude encourages us to look for the good in every situation, fostering resilience and a more optimistic outlook on life.

7. Mindset and Social Engagement

A positive mindset also encourages active social engagement, which is vital for emotional and mental well-being. Individuals with a positive outlook are more likely to seek out social connections, build meaningful relationships, and participate in community activities. These connections provide emotional support, reduce feelings of loneliness, and contribute to a sense of belonging and purpose.

Building Strong Social Networks: By adopting a mindset that values connection and community, we can strengthen our social networks and enrich our lives with meaningful relationships. This engagement fosters a sense of purpose and fulfillment, enhancing our overall quality of life as we age.

The power of mindset in aging gracefully cannot be overstated. A positive, growth-oriented mindset can transform our experience of aging, allowing us to embrace the changes and opportunities that come with growing older. By cultivating a mindset that values learning, resilience, gratitude, and connection, we can navigate the aging process with grace, confidence, and a sense of purpose. Ultimately, our mindset shapes our reality, and by choosing to see aging as a natural, enriching, and empowering part of life, we can age gracefully and joyfully on purpose.

Finding Purpose in Later Life: By cultivating a mindset that values purpose and contribution, we can continue to find meaning in our lives as we age. Whether through volunteering, mentoring, creative pursuits, or simply being present for loved ones, finding ways to give back and stay engaged can help us live with greater intention and joy. The power of mindset in shaping the aging experience is profound. A positive, growthoriented mindset can help us embrace the aging process with resilience, optimism, and a sense of purpose. By choosing to see aging as an opportunity for continued growth, learning, and connection, we can navigate the changes of later life with grace and confidence. Ultimately, our mindset determines how we experience aging, and by cultivating a positive and empowered mindset, we can live fully and joyfully at every stage of life.

Chapter 3. Self-Care and Wellness: Nurturing Mind, Body, and Spirit in the Aging Process

As we age, taking care of ourselves becomes more important than ever. Self-care and wellness are essential components of aging gracefully, helping us maintain our physical health, mental clarity, and emotional balance. By prioritizing self-care, we can enhance our quality of life, increase our longevity, and embrace the aging process with vitality and joy.

1. The Importance of Self-Care in Aging

Self-care is the practice of taking deliberate actions to preserve or improve one's health and well-being. It involves recognizing our needs—physical, emotional, mental, and spiritual—and taking proactive steps to meet them. As we age, our bodies and minds undergo changes that require us to be more mindful of how we care for ourselves. Effective self-care can help us:

- **Maintain Physical Health:** Regular exercise, proper nutrition, and adequate sleep are foundational to physical health. These practices help maintain strength, flexibility, and stamina, reduce the risk of chronic diseases, and promote overall vitality.

- **Support Mental and Emotional Well-being:** Activities that reduce stress, promote relaxation, and foster a positive outlook are essential for mental and emotional health. This includes practices such as mindfulness, meditation, and engaging in hobbies or activities that bring joy and fulfillment.
- **Enhance Cognitive Function:** Staying mentally active through lifelong learning, puzzles, reading, or engaging in new activities can help maintain cognitive function and reduce the risk of cognitive decline.
- **Nurture Spiritual Health:** For many, spiritual practices such as prayer, meditation, or community worship provide comfort, guidance, and a sense of purpose.

2. Physical Self-Care: Keeping the Body Strong and Healthy

Maintaining physical health is a crucial aspect of aging gracefully. As we age, our bodies change, and it becomes even more important to engage in regular physical activity, eat a balanced diet, and get sufficient rest.

- **Exercise Regularly:** Engaging in regular physical activity is vital for maintaining strength, flexibility, and cardiovascular health. Activities such as walking, swimming, yoga, or strength training can help improve balance, coordination, and endurance, reducing the risk of falls and injuries. Exercise also releases endorphins, which enhance mood and promote emotional well-being.
- **Eat a Balanced Diet:** Nutrition plays a key role in overall health and well-being. A diet rich in fruits, vegetables, lean proteins, whole grains, and healthy fats can provide essential nutrients that support bodily functions, boost immunity, and reduce the risk of chronic conditions such as heart disease, diabetes, and osteoporosis. Staying hydrated is also essential for maintaining energy levels and supporting cognitive function.
- **Prioritize Rest and Sleep:** Quality sleep is essential for physical and mental health. As we age, sleep patterns may change, making it important to establish a regular sleep routine and create a restful environment. Adequate sleep supports the immune system, enhances memory and concentration, and improves mood and overall well-being.

3. Emotional and Mental Self-Care: Fostering Resilience and Positivity

Emotional and mental self-care involves practices that help us manage stress, build resilience, and maintain a positive outlook on life. It's about nurturing our inner world and ensuring we stay emotionally balanced and mentally sharp.

- **Practice Mindfulness and Meditation:** Mindfulness and meditation can help reduce stress, enhance emotional regulation, and improve mental clarity. These practices encourage us to stay present, develop self-awareness, and respond to life's challenges with calm and grace.
- **Stay Socially Connected:** Maintaining social connections is vital for emotional well-being. Engaging with family, friends, or community groups can provide emotional support, reduce feelings of loneliness, and enhance a sense of belonging. Building and maintaining meaningful relationships contribute to a richer, more fulfilling life.
- **Engage in Lifelong Learning:** Keeping the mind active through lifelong learning is crucial for cognitive health. Activities like reading, taking up a new hobby, playing

musical instruments, or learning a new language can help maintain cognitive function, boost memory, and enhance mental agility.

- **Practice Gratitude and Positivity:** Cultivating an attitude of gratitude and positivity can significantly impact emotional well-being. Keeping a gratitude journal, reflecting on positive experiences, or expressing appreciation to others can foster a positive outlook on life, enhancing resilience and overall happiness.

4. Spiritual Self-Care: Connecting with Inner Peace and Purpose

For many, spiritual self-care is a fundamental aspect of aging gracefully. It involves nurturing the soul and seeking meaning, purpose, and connection beyond the self. ● **Engage in Spiritual Practices:** Practices such as prayer, meditation, or attending religious services can provide comfort, guidance, and a sense of connection to a higher power. Spirituality often offers a framework for understanding life's challenges and finding peace amid uncertainty.

- **Connect with Nature:** Nature has a profound ability to restore the soul and provide a sense of peace and renewal. Spending time outdoors, whether walking in a park, gardening, or simply sitting in a peaceful natural setting, can enhance spiritual well-being and promote inner calm.

- **Pursue Meaningful Activities:** Engaging in activities that align with personal values and beliefs can provide a sense of purpose and fulfillment. Volunteering, mentoring, or participating in community service can foster a sense of contribution and positively impact both the individual and the community.

5. Creating a Personalized Self-Care Routine

A personalized self-care routine is essential for addressing individual needs and promoting holistic well-being. It involves identifying what activities and practices bring joy, relaxation, and fulfillment and incorporating them into daily life.

- **Assess Personal Needs:** Consider the areas of your life that require attention—physical health, emotional balance, mental stimulation, or spiritual fulfillment. Reflect on what activities make you feel good and what aspects of your well-being need more support.

- **Set Realistic Goals:** Start small and set achievable self-care goals. Whether it's walking for 30 minutes a day, practicing mindfulness for 10 minutes each morning, or calling a friend once a week, setting realistic goals helps build consistency and encourages long-term commitment to self-care.

- **Create a Routine:** Incorporate self-care activities into your daily routine. Schedule time for exercise, relaxation, social activities, and spiritual practices, and make self-care a non-negotiable part of your day.

- **Be Flexible and Adapt:** Be willing to adapt your self-care routine as your needs change. What works at one stage of life may need adjustment as you age. Stay open to trying new activities or modifying existing routines to better suit your current needs.

6. The Benefits of Self-Care and Wellness

Prioritizing self-care and wellness offer numerous benefits that enhance the aging process: ● **Improved Physical Health:** Regular self-care practices help maintain physical health, reduce the risk of chronic diseases, and promote longevity.

- **Enhanced Emotional and Mental Well-Being:** Self-care fosters resilience, reduces stress, and enhances emotional stability and mental clarity.
- **Greater Life Satisfaction:** Engaging in activities that bring joy and fulfillment can increase overall life satisfaction and a sense of purpose.
- **Increased Self-Esteem and Confidence:** Taking care of oneself promotes a positive self-image and boosts confidence, helping individuals navigate the aging process with grace and self-assurance.

Self-care and wellness are vital for aging gracefully and maintaining a high quality of life. By prioritizing physical, emotional, mental, and spiritual self-care, we can nurture our whole selves and embrace the aging process with vitality and joy. Remember, self-care is not a luxury but a necessity for well-being at every stage of life. By committing to a personalized self-care routine, we can empower ourselves to age with grace, resilience, and a deep sense of fulfillment.

The Importance of Self-Acceptance: Embracing the Aging Process

Self-acceptance is a crucial component of aging gracefully. As we age, we are confronted with various physical, emotional, and social changes that can challenge our sense of identity and self-worth. Embracing these changes with self-acceptance can lead to a more fulfilling and meaningful experience of aging. **1. Recognizing the Power of Self-Acceptance**

Self-acceptance means recognizing and embracing who we are at every stage of life, including the changes that come with aging. It involves acknowledging our strengths, weaknesses, and the unique experiences that have shaped us. By practicing selfacceptance, we learn to love ourselves unconditionally, regardless of societal standards or expectations. This mindset shift is essential for aging gracefully because it allows us to focus on what truly matters: our inner growth, relationships, and overall well-being.

2. Embracing Physical Changes

One of the most visible aspects of aging is the physical changes our bodies undergo. Wrinkles, gray hair, changes in body shape, and reduced physical capabilities are natural parts of growing older. Society often places a high value on youth and beauty, leading many to feel insecure or dissatisfied with their appearance as they age.

The Role of Self-Acceptance: By practicing self-acceptance, we can shift our perspective from focusing on physical appearance to appreciating our bodies for their strength, resilience, and the journey they have carried us through. Instead of resisting or denying these changes, we can embrace them as a testament to our life experiences and the wisdom we have gained. This acceptance helps reduce anxiety and fosters a positive selfimage, allowing us to celebrate the aging process rather than fear it.

3. Appreciating Emotional and Psychological Growth

Aging is not just a physical journey; it is also an emotional and psychological one. As we age, we often develop greater emotional intelligence, resilience, and a deeper understanding of ourselves and others. These qualities can lead to more meaningful relationships, a stronger sense of purpose, and a greater capacity for empathy and compassion.

The Role of Self-Acceptance: Accepting ourselves as we are allows us to fully appreciate the emotional and psychological growth that comes with age. We learn to value the lessons learned from our experiences, both positive and negative, and understand that each stage of life brings its own set of opportunities for personal development. By embracing this growth, we can approach aging with a sense of fulfillment and gratitude, rather than regret or fear.

4. Letting Go of Societal Expectations

Societal pressures and stereotypes about aging can create unrealistic expectations about what it means to grow older. These pressures can lead to feelings of inadequacy, fear, or the desire to resist the aging process.

The Role of Self-Acceptance: Self-acceptance encourages us to let go of these external pressures and define aging on our own terms. It empowers us to focus on our own values, desires, and goals, rather than trying to conform to societal standards. This freedom allows us to live authentically and fully, embracing our unique path and the gifts that come with each stage of life.

5. Finding Joy in the Present Moment

Aging often brings about a greater appreciation for the present moment. As we recognize the finite nature of life, we may become more inclined to cherish each day and find joy in simple pleasures.

The Role of Self-Acceptance: By accepting ourselves and our current stage of life, we are more likely to find peace and contentment in the present moment. We become less focused on the past or anxious about the future and more engaged in the here and now. This mindfulness can enhance our overall well-being and lead to a more joyful and fulfilling experience of aging.

6. Cultivating a Positive Mindset

A positive mindset is essential for embracing the aging process. It involves focusing on what we can control—our attitudes, behaviors, and reactions—rather than what we cannot, such as the passage of time.

The Role of Self-Acceptance: Self-acceptance is the foundation of a positive mindset. It encourages us to view aging not as a decline but as a natural and valuable part of life. By embracing our true selves and accepting the changes that come with aging, we can cultivate a sense of peace, resilience, and optimism that enhances our quality of life.

Embracing the aging process with self-acceptance is key to aging gracefully. It allows us to honor our journey, appreciate the growth and wisdom that come with age, and find joy and fulfillment in every stage of life. By letting go of societal expectations, celebrating our physical and emotional changes, and cultivating a positive mindset, we can transform the experience of aging into a powerful and enriching chapter of our lives. **Chapter 4. Self-Reflection Exercise: Embracing Aging and Personal Growth 1. Reflect on Your Life's Journey:**

- **Questions:** o What are the most significant milestones in your life? o How have these experiences shaped who you are today? o What lessons have you learned from both positive and challenging experiences?

- **Action:** o Write down these milestones and lessons in a journal. Consider how each has contributed to your personal growth.

2. Assess Your Current State:

- **Questions:** o How do you feel about where you are in life right now? o What are the aspects of your life that you are most grateful for? o Are there areas in your life that you feel need improvement or change?
- **Action:** o List out the areas where you feel content and those where you would like to see growth. Reflect on what changes you can make to improve those areas.

3. Identify Core Values:

- **Questions:** o What values have guided your decisions and actions throughout your life? o Are there any values that have become more important to you as you've aged? o How can you align your daily actions with these core values?
- **Action:**

o Create a list of your core values and write a brief statement on how you will honor each value in your daily life.

4. Envision Your Future:

- **Questions:** o What does personal growth mean to you at this stage of life? o How do you envision your future self in the next 5, 10, or 20 years? o What new skills, knowledge, or experiences would you like to pursue?
- **Action:** o Write a letter to your future self, describing the person you hope to become. o Outline specific goals for personal growth and steps you can take to achieve them.

5. Cultivate Gratitude and Positivity: • Questions: o What are you most grateful for in your life? o How can you practice gratitude daily to enhance your sense of fulfillment?

o What positive affirmations can you incorporate into your routine to support your personal growth?

- **Action:**

o Start a daily gratitude journal, listing at least three things you are grateful for each day.
o Pair this with positive affirmations that resonate with your personal growth journey.

6. Embrace Change and Let Go:

- **Questions:** o What are you holding onto that no longer serves you? o How can you practice acceptance and let go of past regrets or disappointments? o How can you embrace the changes that come with aging in a positive way?
- **Action:**

o Identify one thing you are ready to let go of and create a symbolic gesture (e.g., writing it down and tearing up the paper) to signify this release. Reflect on how this will create space for new growth.

Aging brings unique opportunities for self-reflection and personal growth. By engaging in this exercise, you can gain deeper insights into your life's journey, align with your core values, and set meaningful goals for the future. Embracing aging as a time of continued growth and fulfillment can lead to a richer, more purposeful life.

Chapter 5. Understanding Emotional Resilience and Mental Health in Aging Emotional Resilience:

Emotional resilience refers to the ability to adapt to stressful situations and recover quickly from adversity, trauma, or setbacks. It is a key component of mental health and well-being, especially as one ages. Emotional resilience is not about avoiding difficulties but rather developing the capacity to cope with life's challenges in a healthy, balanced way.

Key Aspects of Emotional Resilience:

1. **Adaptability:**

o The ability to adjust to new circumstances or changes, such as retirement, loss of loved ones, or changes in physical health. o Staying open to new experiences and being flexible in one's approach to life.

2. **Positive Mindset:**

o Maintaining a positive outlook and finding meaning or lessons in life's challenges. o Focusing on what can be controlled and letting go of what cannot be changed.

3. **Self-Compassion:**

o Being kind to oneself in times of failure or pain rather than being overly critical. o Recognizing that struggles are a universal human experience.

4. **Emotional Regulation:**

o Developing the ability to manage and respond to emotional experiences effectively. o Using techniques like mindfulness, meditation, or deep breathing to stay calm and centered.

5. **Social Support:**

o Cultivating a strong support network of friends, family, and community.

o Being willing to seek help and talk about emotions with trusted individuals or professionals.

Mental Health in Aging:

Mental health encompasses emotional, psychological, and social well-being. It affects how people think, feel, and act, especially in how they handle stress, relate to others, and make choices. As people age, maintaining good mental health is crucial for a high quality of life.

Key Considerations for Mental Health in Aging:

1.　　**Cognitive Health:** o Engaging in activities that stimulate the mind, such as puzzles, reading, learning new skills, or playing musical instruments. o Preventing cognitive decline through regular mental exercises and maintaining a healthy lifestyle.

2.　　**Managing Stress and Anxiety:** o Recognizing sources of stress and developing healthy coping mechanisms, such as regular physical activity, hobbies, or relaxation techniques.

o Avoiding isolation, which can exacerbate feelings of anxiety or depression.

3. **Emotional Well-being:**

o Acknowledging and expressing feelings in healthy ways, rather than suppressing them.

o Fostering a sense of purpose through volunteering, mentoring, or other meaningful activities.

4.　　**Depression and Loneliness:** o Being aware of the signs of depression, which may include persistent sadness, loss of interest in activities, changes in appetite or sleep, and difficulty concentrating. o Addressing loneliness by staying socially active and connected with others.

5.   **Grief and Loss:** o Learning to process and cope with grief related to the loss of loved ones, declining health, or other significant life changes. o Understanding that grief is a natural part of life and finding ways to honor lost relationships or abilities.

Strategies to Enhance Emotional Resilience and Mental Health:

1. **Mindfulness and Meditation:**

o Practicing mindfulness techniques to stay present and manage stress. o Meditation can help regulate emotions and increase self-awareness.

2. **Healthy Lifestyle Choices:** o Maintaining a balanced diet, regular exercise, and adequate sleep to support overall mental health.

o Avoiding substances like alcohol or drugs, which can negatively impact mental well-being.

3.   **Building Strong Relationships:** o Engaging in regular social activities and maintaining strong connections with family and friends. o Joining community groups or support networks to build a sense of belonging.

4.   **Seeking Professional Help:** o Consulting with mental health professionals, such as therapists or counselors, for support when needed.

o Participating in support groups for individuals facing similar life challenges.

5. **Continuous Learning and Growth:**

o Encouraging lifelong learning and personal development to stay mentally engaged. o Setting new goals and pursuing hobbies or interests that bring joy and fulfillment.

By fostering emotional resilience and taking proactive steps to maintain mental health, older adults can navigate the aging process with greater ease, purpose, and joy.

Chapter 6. Navigating Relationship Challenges

Relationship challenges are inevitable, they can be navigated successfully with the right tools and mindset. Maintaining strong, meaningful connections throughout your lives will help you to adjust to changes later in life

Relationships are dynamic and evolve over time, especially as we age. We can acknowledge that aging can bring specific challenges to relationships, such as changes in social roles, loss of loved ones, and evolving needs. So, we emphasize the importance of resilience, adaptability, and proactive strategies in maintaining healthy relationships.

1. **Coping with Loss (we will explore a whole section on grief later in the chapter)** •
    Understanding Grief and Its Impact on Relationships: The grieving process and its different stages can affect relationships with friends, family, and even oneself. •
    Finding Support Systems: By joining support groups, either locally or online, where individuals can share their experiences with others who understand what they are going through.
        • **Honoring the Memory of Loved Ones**: We can honor and remember loved ones, such as creating a memory book, planting a tree, or engaging in activities they loved. •

Maintaining Open Communication: Communicating openly with loved ones about feelings of grief and loss to avoid misunderstandings and provide mutual support.

2. Managing Loneliness

- **Recognizing the Signs of Loneliness**: Loneliness can introduce feelings of sadness, withdrawal, or a lack of motivation to engage in social activities.
- **Creating a Plan for Social Engagement**: Look for ways to actively engage with others, such as scheduling regular meetups, participating in group activities, or even taking up new hobbies that involve social interaction.
- **Utilizing Technology to Stay Connected**: Technology, such as video calls and social media, can help bridge the gap and maintain connections with friends and family, especially when physical proximity is not possible.
- **Adopting a Pet**: Pet ownership for companionship, particularly for those who live alone can provide emotional support and a sense of routine and purpose.

3. Dealing with Changes in Social Roles

- **Adjusting to Retirement**: There are emotional and social adjustments required when retiring, such as finding new ways to define one's identity and purpose without the daily structure of work.
- **Redefining Purpose and Identity**: Explore new roles and activities that bring meaning and satisfaction, such as volunteering, mentoring, or engaging in creative pursuits.
- **Maintaining a Sense of Purpose**: Stay engaged and purposeful in retirement, such as setting personal goals, continuing to learn, or contributing to the community in meaningful ways.
- **Navigating Changes in Family Dynamics**: Aging can change family dynamics, such as becoming a grandparent or adjusting to adult children becoming more independent or taking on caregiving roles.

4. Resolving Conflicts and Misunderstandings

- **Effective Communication Techniques**: Effective communication skills, such as active listening, expressing feelings without blame, and using "I" statements to express concerns or needs.
- **Practicing Empathy and Understanding**: Practice empathy and try to understand the perspectives of others to help resolve conflicts.

-
    Seeking Mediation or Counseling: Seek professional help, such as mediation or counseling, for unresolved or particularly challenging conflicts.
- **Learning to Let Go and Forgive**: It is important to forgive and let go of grudges to maintain healthy and fulfilling relationships.

5. Overcoming Health-Related Relationship Struggles

- **Communicating Health Needs and Boundaries**: Maintain open communication about health issues and how they may affect relationships. This includes setting boundaries and asking for support when needed.
- **Supporting a Partner with Health Challenges**: Support a partner with health issues, such as being patient, educating oneself about their condition, and finding a balance between caregiving and maintaining personal well-being.
- **Dealing with Caregiver Stress**: There are challenges faced by caregivers, including emotional, physical, and mental exhaustion, it helps when you learn to manage stress and seek support.

6. Navigating Cultural and Generational Differences

- **Bridging Generational Gaps**: Different generations may have different perspectives and values; we can bridge these gaps through open dialogue and mutual respect.
- **Celebrating Diversity**: Embrace and celebrate cultural differences within relationships to enrich and deepen connections.
- **Finding Common Ground**: Look for common interests or values that can serve as a foundation for building stronger intergenerational or culturally diverse relationships.

7. Building Resilience in Relationships

- **Understanding Emotional Resilience**: Emotional resilience helps individuals navigate relationship challenges more effectively.
- **Developing Healthy Coping Mechanisms**: Healthy coping strategies, such as mindfulness, meditation, or journaling, help to manage emotional stress within relationships.
- **Practicing Patience and Flexibility**: It is important to be patient and flexible in adapting to changes and challenges in relationships.

8. Fostering Independence While Maintaining Connections

- **Balancing Independence with Interdependence**: Maintain a sense of independence while still nurturing close relationships.
- **Encouraging Self-Care for Both Partners**: Self-care for both maintains personal well-being, which in turn strengthens relationships.
- **Setting Healthy Boundaries**: Setting and respecting boundaries in relationships to ensure mutual respect and understanding is critical.

9. Cultivating a Growth Mindset in Relationships

- **Viewing Challenges as Opportunities for Growth**: Relationship challenges provide opportunities to learn, grow, and strengthen bonds.

-
- **Embracing Change and Adaptation**: Be open to change and adapt to new circumstances in relationships.

    Learning from Mistakes and Moving Forward: Learning from past mistakes and focusing on positively moving forward in relationships.

The Grieving Process

The grieving process can be one of the most difficult times in our relationships. Grief is a natural response to loss, whether it is the death of a loved one, the end of a significant relationship, or other major life changes. Grief can deeply impact an individual's emotions, thoughts, and behaviors, often affecting their relationships with others. Understanding the grieving process and its effects on relationships can help individuals navigate this challenging time with compassion and support.

Grief introduces a whole different type of relationship challenges. Grief is a highly personal experience that varies greatly from person to person. While there is no "right" way to grieve, several models attempt to describe the common stages people may go through. One of the most well-known models is the **Five Stages of Grief** developed by Elisabeth Kübler-Ross. It's important to note that not everyone will experience all of these stages, nor will they necessarily occur in a linear order.

The Five Stages of Grief:

1. **Denial**: This initial stage often serves as a defense mechanism to help cope with the shock of the loss. The person might struggle to accept the reality of what has happened, which can manifest as disbelief, numbness, or feeling as if they are in a dream.
2. **Anger**: As the denial fades, it is often replaced by feelings of frustration, anger, and helplessness. Individuals may direct their anger towards themselves, others, or even the person they have lost. They might feel abandoned or question why the loss happened to them.
3. **Bargaining**: In this stage, individuals may try to regain control or find meaning in their loss. They might reflect on "what if" scenarios, wish they had acted differently, or make promises to a higher power in hopes of reversing the loss or alleviating their pain.
4. **Depression**: During this stage, the full weight of the loss may begin to sink in, leading to feelings of sadness, despair, and hopelessness. This is often the most challenging stage emotionally, as the person confronts the reality of their loss and its impact on their life.
5. **Acceptance**: In this stage, individuals begin to come to terms with their loss. Acceptance does not mean the person is "over" their grief but rather that they have found a way to live with it. They may start to make peace with their new reality and find ways to move forward.

How Grief Affects Relationships

Grieving can significantly impact an individual's relationships, often in complex and sometimes contradictory ways. The effects of grief on relationships depend on various factors, including the nature of the loss, the individual's coping mechanisms, and the dynamics of their relationships before the loss. Here are some common ways grief can affect relationships:

•

1. Changes in Communication Patterns

Withdrawing or Isolating: Grieving individuals may withdraw from social interactions and isolate themselves. They might feel overwhelmed by their emotions or unable to communicate their feelings effectively. This withdrawal can lead to a breakdown in communication with friends and family members, potentially causing misunderstandings or feelings of rejection.

• **Oversharing or Seeking Constant Support**: Conversely, some individuals may seek constant support and repeatedly talk about their loss, which can be challenging for friends and family members who may not know how to respond or provide adequate support.

2. Shifts in Emotional Dynamics

• **Increased Sensitivity**: Grief can make individuals more sensitive or reactive, leading to emotional outbursts or conflicts in relationships. They may be easily triggered by comments or actions that remind them of their loss, causing strain in their relationships.

• **Role Reversal**: If a grieving individual was previously the primary source of emotional support for others, the dynamics might shift as they become the one needing support. This role reversal can be challenging for both parties, especially if the person providing support is not used to being in that role.

3. Strained Intimacy and Closeness

• **Reduced Physical and Emotional Intimacy**: Grief can diminish a person's desire for physical or emotional intimacy. They may feel disconnected from their partner or lack the energy to engage in affectionate behaviors, potentially causing strain in romantic relationships.

• **Differing Grieving Styles**: Partners may grieve differently, leading to misunderstandings or feelings of alienation. For example, one partner may want to talk about the loss and express their feelings, while the other may prefer to process their grief privately.

4. Conflicts and Misunderstandings

• **Increased Conflicts**: The heightened emotions that come with grief can lead to increased conflicts in relationships. Misunderstandings may arise when one person feels the other is not providing adequate support or is not grieving "appropriately." • **Misplaced Anger or Frustration**: Individuals in the anger stage of grief may direct their anger or frustration towards those closest to them, including friends and family. This can cause tension and conflict in relationships, even if the anger is not directly related to the relationship itself.

5. Strengthening or Weakening Bonds

• **Strengthening Bonds**: For some, grief can strengthen bonds with loved ones as they come together to support each other and navigate their loss collectively. Sharing memories, emotions, and providing mutual support can deepen connections and foster a sense of solidarity.

-
- **Weakening Bonds**: For others, grief may strain or weaken relationships if the support they need is not forthcoming or if friends and family members are uncomfortable or unsure how to provide support. If the grieving person feels misunderstood or unsupported, it can create distance or resentment.

6 Changes in Social Roles and Responsibilities

- **Assuming New Roles**: Grief can also bring about changes in social roles and responsibilities. For example, a person may need to take on caregiving duties for a surviving loved one, or they may need to manage the financial and logistical aspects of the loss. These new roles can create additional stress and affect relationships. •
- **Impact on Social Networks**: The loss of a loved one can impact a person's broader social network, such as losing a key social organizer or a central figure in a group. This can lead to a sense of disconnection from the group or a reevaluation of social ties.

Strategies for Navigating Grief in Relationships

1. **Open and Honest Communication**: Encourage open and honest communication with loved ones about feelings and needs during the grieving process. Sharing one's experience and being transparent about what kind of support is helpful can foster understanding and reduce misunderstandings.
2. **Seek Professional Support**: Consider seeking professional support from a therapist, counselor, or grief support group. Professionals can provide a safe space to express emotions and offer strategies to navigate grief's impact on relationships.
3. **Set Boundaries**: Setting boundaries is crucial when grieving, both for oneself and for others. It's okay to say no to social invitations or to take time alone if needed. Similarly, understanding and respecting others' boundaries during this time is important.
4. **Practice Patience and Empathy**: Grief is a complex and often lengthy process. Practicing patience with oneself and others can help navigate the ups and downs. Showing empathy and trying to understand that everyone grieves differently can also foster compassion and connection.
5. **Find Meaning Together**: Engage in activities that honor the memory of the deceased or the loss experienced. This could include creating a memorial, participating in a charity walk, or simply sharing stories and memories with loved ones.
6. **Focus on Self-Care**: Encourage both the grieving individual and their loved ones to focus on self-care. Grieving can be physically and emotionally draining, so prioritizing rest, nutrition, exercise, and relaxation can help maintain overall wellbeing.
7. **Rebuild Social Connections**: When ready, gradually rebuild social connections by participating in social activities, joining clubs or groups, or volunteering. Engaging in community activities can provide a sense of purpose and belonging.

By understanding the grieving process and its impact on relationships, individuals can better navigate this challenging time, fostering resilience and maintaining meaningful connections with loved ones. **1. Cultivate Meaningful Connections**

- **Rekindle Old Friendships**: Reach out to old friends or acquaintances. A simple phone call, text, or email can help reestablish connections that may have faded over time. Sharing memories and experiences can reignite bonds and provide a sense of continuity and comfort.
- **Join Social Groups or Clubs**: Participate in social clubs or groups that align with personal interests, such as book clubs, hobby groups, religious organizations, or

community centers. Engaging in regular group activities fosters a sense of belonging and provides opportunities to meet new people.

- **Volunteer in the Community**: Volunteering can provide a sense of purpose and connection to others. Helping those in need or contributing to community projects can create meaningful relationships and reduce feelings of loneliness. It also shifts the focus from one's own loneliness to the needs of others.
- **Use Technology to Stay Connected**: Leverage technology to stay in touch with friends and family, especially if they live far away. Video calls, social media, and messaging apps can help maintain relationships and provide real-time interaction. Virtual events or online communities can also offer a platform for social engagement.
- **Consider Intergenerational Activities**: Engaging in activities with younger generations, such as mentoring programs or family activities, can provide fresh perspectives and a sense of purpose. Intergenerational relationships can be mutually beneficial, offering support, knowledge exchange, and emotional fulfillment.

2. Develop a Routine and Stay Active

- **Establish a Daily Routine**: Creating a structured daily routine helps provide a sense of purpose and normalcy. Incorporating activities like exercise, hobbies, social interactions, and self-care into the daily routine can prevent feelings of aimlessness and isolation.
- **Engage in Regular Physical Activity**: Physical activity can boost mood, reduce stress, and promote overall well-being. Join a local exercise class, such as yoga, tai chi, or swimming, that accommodates different fitness levels and provides an opportunity for social interaction.
- **Participate in Group Exercise Classes**: Group exercise classes not only promote physical health but also provide a social setting where individuals can meet others with similar interests. Classes such as dance, yoga, or water aerobics are great for socializing while staying active.
- **Pursue Hobbies and Interests**: Engaging in hobbies and interests can provide a sense of fulfillment and joy. Whether it's gardening, painting, playing a musical instrument, or learning a new skill, pursuing personal passions helps maintain mental stimulation and provides opportunities for social engagement.

3. Practice Mindfulness and Self-Reflection

- **Mindfulness and Meditation**: Practice mindfulness and meditation to cultivate a sense of inner peace and self-awareness. Mindfulness techniques, such as deep breathing, meditation, and journaling, can help manage feelings of loneliness by fostering a sense of calm and acceptance.
- **Reflect on Personal Strengths and Achievements**: Reflect on past achievements, skills, and strengths. This practice can boost self-esteem and provide motivation to pursue new goals and activities. Recognizing one's value and contributions can mitigate feelings of loneliness and self-doubt.
- **Focus on Self-Care and Well-Being**: Prioritize self-care activities that nurture the body and mind, such as healthy eating, adequate sleep, and regular exercise. Taking

care of oneself physically and emotionally can improve overall well-being and create a more positive outlook on life.

4. Foster a Positive Mindset

- **Adopt a Growth Mindset**: Embrace a growth mindset by viewing loneliness as an opportunity for personal growth and self-discovery. Rather than seeing loneliness as a negative state, consider it a chance to learn more about oneself, develop new skills, and explore new interests.

- **Set Realistic and Achievable Goals**: Setting small, achievable goals can provide a sense of purpose and accomplishment. These goals could be related to social interactions, personal growth, or learning new skills. Achieving these goals can boost self-confidence and encourage further engagement.

- **Reframe Negative Thoughts**: Practice reframing negative thoughts about loneliness into more positive or neutral perspectives. Instead of thinking, "I'm alone," try thinking, "I'm taking this time to focus on myself and explore new interests."

5. Seek Professional Support and Counseling

- **Therapy and Counseling**: Consider seeking professional support from a therapist or counselor. Therapy can provide a safe space to explore feelings of loneliness, develop coping strategies, and address any underlying mental health issues, such as depression or anxiety.

- **Join Support Groups**: Support groups offer a platform to connect with others who may be experiencing similar feelings of loneliness or isolation. Sharing experiences and providing mutual support can foster a sense of belonging and understanding.

6. Engage in Meaningful Activities

- **Pursue Lifelong Learning**: Engage in lifelong learning by taking classes or attending workshops on subjects of interest. Learning new things keeps the mind active and provides opportunities to meet new people with similar interests. • **Create Art or Engage in Creative Activities**: Creative activities, such as painting, writing, crafting, or playing music, can be therapeutic and provide a sense of accomplishment. Sharing these activities with others or joining creative groups can also foster social connections.

7. Explore Spirituality and Faith

- **Join a Faith-Based Community**: Participate in faith-based activities or join a spiritual community. Many people find comfort, purpose, and community through religious or spiritual practices. Attending services, participating in study groups, or engaging in community outreach programs can provide a sense of belonging and connection.

- **Practice Gratitude and Reflection**: Incorporate gratitude practices, such as keeping a gratitude journal or reflecting on daily blessings. Focusing on positive aspects of life can shift the focus away from loneliness and promote a more optimistic outlook.

8. Consider Pet Companionship

- **Adopt a Pet**: Pets can provide companionship, emotional support, and a sense of purpose. Caring for a pet can reduce feelings of loneliness, encourage regular physical activity, and provide a routine. Pets can also be a great conversation starter, facilitating social interactions with other pet owners.

- **Participate in Pet Therapy Programs**: If owning a pet is not feasible, consider participating in pet therapy programs. These programs provide opportunities to interact with therapy animals, which can be comforting and uplifting.

9. Embrace Nature and Outdoor Activities

- **Spend Time in Nature**: Spending time outdoors can have a positive impact on mental well-being. Activities like walking in a park, gardening, or simply sitting in a natural setting can reduce feelings of loneliness and improve mood.

- **Join Outdoor Groups**: Participate in outdoor activities with others, such as walking groups, hiking clubs, or community gardening projects. Engaging in nature based activities with others fosters social connections and promotes physical and mental health.

10. Build a Supportive Social Network

- **Identify a Supportive Network**: Identify and cultivate a network of supportive individuals, including friends, family members, neighbors, or community members. Having a reliable support network can provide comfort, encouragement, and companionship during times of loneliness.

- **Attend Social Events and Gatherings**: Attend local events, such as community fairs, cultural festivals, or neighborhood gatherings. These events provide opportunities to meet new people, engage in conversations, and build social connections.

Managing loneliness requires a combination of self-awareness, proactive social engagement, and self-care. By cultivating meaningful connections, engaging in fulfilling activities, and fostering a positive mindset, individuals can reduce feelings of loneliness and enhance their overall quality of life. Remember that it is normal to feel lonely at times, and reaching out for support and connection can make a significant difference in one's emotional and mental well-being.

1. Embrace the Transition

- **Acknowledge the Change**: Accepting that change is a natural part of life can help ease the emotional burden of shifting roles. Recognizing the new phase of life can create space for new opportunities and experiences.

- **Reflect on the Past**: Take time to reflect on past roles and their contributions to one's identity and purpose. Celebrate achievements and contributions made in previous roles, acknowledging the value they brought to oneself and others. ● **Stay Open to New Roles**: Being open to taking on new roles, whether within the family, community, or personal life, can provide a sense of purpose and fulfillment. This might include becoming a mentor, a volunteer, or a leader in community organizations.

2. Stay Connected with Family and Friends

- **Maintain Family Roles**: While the dynamics may shift, continue to engage in meaningful family roles, such as being a supportive grandparent, an advisor to adult children, or a cherished sibling. Regular communication and involvement in family activities help maintain these important relationships.

- **Build a Strong Social Network**: Cultivate relationships with friends and peers who are going through similar life transitions. These connections can provide emotional support, understanding, and companionship, which are crucial during periods of change.
- **Participate in Social Activities**: Join social groups, clubs, or community organizations to stay engaged and build new friendships. Activities such as book clubs, gardening clubs, or religious groups can offer social interaction and a sense of belonging.

3. Find New Purpose and Meaning

- **Volunteer and Give Back**: Volunteering provides an opportunity to contribute to the community and offers a new sense of purpose. Many organizations welcome the experience and wisdom of older volunteers in roles such as tutoring, mentoring, or helping with community projects.
- **Pursue Lifelong Learning**: Engaging in lifelong learning, such as taking classes at a local college or community center, can provide intellectual stimulation and a sense of achievement. Learning new skills or exploring new interests can help redefine one's purpose in later years.
- **Mentorship and Knowledge Sharing**: Share your experience and wisdom with younger generations. Mentorship can be a fulfilling role, providing guidance and support while helping others navigate their own life challenges and career paths.

4. Adapt to Physical Changes

- **Focus on Abilities, Not Limitations**: Instead of dwelling on what can no longer be done, focus on what is still possible. Adapt activities to match current physical capabilities, ensuring that they remain enjoyable and fulfilling.
- **Stay Physically Active**: Regular physical activity is crucial for maintaining health and independence. Choose activities that are safe and enjoyable, such as walking, yoga, or swimming, to stay active and connected with others.
- **Modify Living Arrangements as Needed**: If mobility or health issues require a change in living arrangements, approach this as a way to maintain independence and ensure safety. Consider options like downsizing to a more manageable home, moving closer to family, or exploring senior living communities that offer social activities and support.

5. Seek Support and Counseling

- **Professional Counseling**: Consider speaking with a counselor or therapist to navigate the emotional aspects of changing social roles. Professional support can provide coping strategies and help in adjusting to new circumstances.
- **Join Support Groups**: Support groups for retirees, widows/widowers, or those facing similar life changes can provide comfort and a sense of community. Sharing experiences with others who understand can help alleviate feelings of isolation and offer new perspectives.

6. Foster a Positive Outlook

- **Practice Gratitude and Mindfulness**: Engage in practices such as gratitude journaling or mindfulness meditation to foster a positive outlook. Focusing on the positive aspects of life and being present in the moment can help reduce anxiety about the future.

- **Cultivate Resilience**: Building resilience involves adapting to changes and finding ways to bounce back from challenges. Focus on strengths and past experiences that have demonstrated the ability to overcome adversity.
- **Reframe Aging as a Time of Growth**: View aging as an opportunity for growth, self-discovery, and the pursuit of new passions. This shift in perspective can help reduce fear or anxiety about changing roles.

7. Stay Involved in the Community

- **Engage in Community Activities**: Participation in community events, local clubs, or civic organizations can help maintain a sense of involvement and contribution. Being active in the community provides a sense of purpose and fosters social connections.
- **Advocate for Change**: Become involved in advocacy work or join groups that work to improve conditions for seniors. This can provide a sense of purpose and the satisfaction of contributing to positive change.

8. Embrace Technology

- **Learn to Use Technology**: Technology can help maintain social connections and provide access to information and entertainment. Learning to use social media, video calls, and messaging apps can help one stay connected with loved ones and the broader community.
- **Participate in Online Communities**: Join online groups or forums that cater to specific interests or hobbies. These communities can provide a sense of belonging and allow for social interaction, especially if mobility is limited.

9. Explore Spiritual and Faith-Based Activities

- **Engage in Spiritual Practices**: Many find comfort and purpose through spiritual or religious practices. Participating in regular worship services, prayer groups, or faith-based community activities can provide support and a sense of belonging. • **Join a Faith-Based Community**: Becoming active in a faith-based community can provide social support, spiritual growth, and opportunities for meaningful engagement with others who share similar values and beliefs.

10. Redefine Success and Fulfillment

- **Set New Goals and Aspirations**: Redefine what success and fulfillment mean in this stage of life. Setting new, realistic goals that align with current abilities and interests can provide motivation and a sense of purpose.
- **Celebrate Achievements**: Acknowledge and celebrate achievements, no matter how small. Recognizing personal accomplishments can boost self-esteem and foster a sense of fulfillment.

Dealing with changes in social roles as one ages involves acceptance, adaptation, and finding new ways to remain engaged and fulfilled. By embracing new opportunities, maintaining social connections, and focusing on personal growth and well-being, older adults can navigate these transitions with resilience and grace. The key is to remain proactive, seek support, and find new ways to contribute to one's community and enjoy life.

Here are some real life people who were able to implement many of the strategies we have been discussing:

1. Martha's Story: Rekindling Old Friendships

"At the age of 65, I found myself feeling a bit lonely after retiring from a busy career as a nurse. I realized that I had lost touch with many old friends over the years. So, I decided to take action. I started reaching out to my high school friends and colleagues, sending them messages and organizing small get-togethers. At first, I was nervous—they might not remember me, or worse, not want to reconnect. But to my surprise, many were delighted to hear from me! We've since rekindled our friendships, and now we have regular coffee meetups and even a yearly reunion trip. It's brought so much joy and companionship back into my life. I've learned that it's never too late to reconnect with those who have meant something to you."

2. James's Experience: Building New Connections Through Volunteering

"After my wife passed away, I struggled with loneliness and a lack of purpose. At 72, I wasn't sure how to fill my days. One day, a neighbor suggested I try volunteering at the local community center. I started helping out with the senior lunch program, and it completely changed my life. Not only did I meet new people who shared similar interests, but I also found a sense of purpose again. The friends I made through volunteering have become like family to me. We support each other, share laughs, and I feel more connected than I have in years. Volunteering taught me that giving back can help you find yourself again, especially in the later stages of life."

3. Sarah's Journey: Embracing Technology to Stay Connected

"As an 80-year-old living alone, I was hesitant to use new technology. But my granddaughter encouraged me to try video calls and social media to stay connected with family and friends. It was intimidating at first, but she patiently taught me how to use my smartphone. Now, I talk to my daughter every day, even though she lives thousands of miles away, and I've joined an online book club where I've met wonderful people from all over the country. Learning to use technology has opened up a whole new world for me. It has allowed me to maintain relationships that I feared I'd lose and even build new ones."

4. Daniel's Reflection: Finding Community in Unexpected Places

"After moving to a new city at 68, I struggled to find a sense of community. I didn't know anyone, and I felt isolated. Then one day, I saw a flyer for a local gardening club. I've always loved gardening, so I decided to give it a try. Joining the club was the best decision I could have made. I met people who shared my passion, and together, we turned an empty plot of land into a beautiful community garden. Now, every Saturday morning is spent with friends who feel like family, and our garden is thriving. I learned that sometimes, community can be found in the most unexpected places—you just have to be open to looking for it."

5. Ruth's Insight: The Power of Forgiveness in Family Relationships

"At 75, I had a strained relationship with my daughter for years. We barely spoke and had unresolved issues that kept us apart. One day, I attended a workshop on forgiveness, and it changed my perspective. I realized that holding onto anger and hurt was only hurting me. I reached out to my daughter, and we began a journey of healing. It wasn't easy, but we talked, cried, and slowly rebuilt our relationship. Now, we speak regularly and spend holidays together. I've learned that forgiveness is a powerful tool for healing and that it's never too late to mend a broken relationship

6. Harry's Movement: Intergenerational Relationships

"As I got older, I realized that many of my peers were moving away or passing on, and I felt a growing sense of isolation. I decided to join a local mentorship program, where older adults paired with younger individuals looking for guidance. I met a young man named Chris, who was struggling with his career path. Over time, we developed a strong bond. I shared my life experiences and helped him navigate his challenges, while he taught me about new technologies and kept me updated on current trends. This intergenerational friendship has been incredibly fulfilling; we both learned and grew from each other. It's taught me that relationships aren't bound by age—there's always something to learn from one another."

7. Jill's Self-love: Exploring yourself

"After my children moved away and my husband passed, I was alone for the first time in 40 years. I spent a long time feeling lost, unsure of who I was without my family around me. I decided to start journaling every morning as a way to connect with myself. Through this process, I discovered passions I had long forgotten—painting, poetry, and even dancing! I began to explore these interests, and not only did I feel more alive, but I also attracted new friends with similar hobbies. I've realized that the most important relationship is the one you have with yourself, and nurturing it opens the door to connecting with others."

8. Anita's Strategy: Creating a Supportive Social Circle

"When my children left for college, and I was nearing retirement, I found myself at a loss for what to do. I knew I needed to create a new social circle to help support this new phase of life. I started by hosting a small potluck dinner with my neighbors. From there, we began a tradition of monthly get-togethers, and soon, a close-knit group formed. We share our joys, struggles, and support each other through life's ups and downs. I've learned that sometimes, taking the first step to bring people together can lead to the most rewarding life."

9. Stephen's Testimony: Opportunities to Be a Light

"Recently, after turning 81 years of age, I had the experience of using 911 to go to Leigh Hospital in Norfolk. After a week there the final diagnosis was pneumonia and lung cancer. Both of my arms had IVs, an oxygen tube was giving needed air to my lungs, and both legs were connected to the foot of my bed pulsating intermittently to prevent blood clots. I suppose I could have grumbled or moaned. But God caused me to rejoice silently inside knowing that it was just another tribulation that brings patience, and patience experience, and experience hope. That hope does not disappoint us because the love of God is shed abroad in our hearts by the Holy Ghost that is given to us. And that is exactly what happened. This whole two-month experience has been opportunity upon opportunity to allow God to let His light shine through me to many others and turn the entire experience into a joyous event. For me growing old isn't just doing it gracefully, it is doing it with purpose and joy."

There are a lot of people who I admire who have lived challenging lives when they were older, these are just two people whose lives impacted my life.

Corrie ten Boom: A Story of Forgiveness, Faith, and Resilience

Corrie ten Boom, a Dutch Christian watchmaker and author, is known for her remarkable story of faith, forgiveness, and resilience during and after World War II. She and her family were arrested by the Nazis for hiding Jews in their home, an act that led to their imprisonment in a concentration camp. Corrie's life is a powerful example of how nurturing the mind and spirit can lead to extraordinary strength and compassion, even in the most harrowing circumstances.

- **Embracing a Growth Mindset Through Forgiveness**: After surviving the horrors of the Ravensbrück concentration camp, Corrie ten Boom emerged with a profound commitment to forgiveness. She traveled the world sharing her story and teaching others about the power of forgiveness and reconciliation. One of her most famous experiences was when she met one of the former Nazi guards who had been particularly cruel to her and her sister. When he asked for her forgiveness, she initially struggled but ultimately chose to forgive him, demonstrating a remarkable capacity for growth and spiritual maturity. This act exemplifies how a growth mindset involves choosing to learn and grow from even the most painful experiences.

- **Faith as a Source of Strength and Resilience**: Corrie's unwavering faith in God was her source of strength throughout her ordeal. She believed that God's love was greater than any evil, and this belief sustained her through unimaginable hardships. After the war, she founded rehabilitation centers for concentration camp survivors and wrote several books that have inspired millions. Her ability to find purpose and meaning in her suffering is a testament to her resilient spirit and growth-oriented mindset.

- **Continuous Spiritual Growth and Sharing Wisdom**: After her release, Corrie ten Boom devoted her life to sharing her experiences and the lessons she learned. She wrote books such as "The Hiding Place," which recounts her story of faith and resilience. Corrie's teachings emphasized that no matter what circumstances one faces, it is always possible to grow spiritually and emotionally. She encouraged people to remain hopeful, maintain their faith, and believe in the transformative power of love and forgiveness.

- **Transforming Trauma into Purpose**: Corrie ten Boom transformed her personal trauma into a mission to help others heal and find peace. By focusing on forgiveness and spiritual growth, she turned her suffering into a source of strength and wisdom. Her story illustrates how a growth mindset allows individuals to transcend their circumstances and find purpose, even in the face of profound adversity.

Exercises and Reflections Inspired by Corrie ten Boom Exercise 1: Forgiveness Meditation

Objective: To cultivate a spirit of forgiveness, inspired by Corrie ten Boom's ability to forgive even her enemies.

1. **Find a Comfortable Position**: Sit comfortably in a quiet place where you won't be disturbed.
2. **Focus on Your Breathing**: Take a few deep breaths, inhaling deeply and exhaling slowly. Allow yourself to relax with each breath.

3. **Visualize Someone You Need to Forgive**: Bring to mind someone you have struggled to forgive. This could be someone from your past or present. Visualize this person in your mind's eye.
4. **Acknowledge Your Feelings**: Notice any feelings of anger, hurt, or resentment that arise. Allow yourself to feel these emotions without judgment.
5. **Send Compassion to Yourself**: Place a hand on your heart and silently say, "May I be free from pain and suffering. May I find peace and forgiveness." Repeat this several times.
6. **Send Compassion to the Other Person**: When you feel ready, extend this compassion to the person you wish to forgive. Silently say, "May you be free from pain and suffering. May you find peace and forgiveness." Repeat this several times.
7. **Release and Reflect**: After a few minutes, gently release the visualization and return your focus to your breathing. Reflect on how the practice felt. Did you notice any shifts in your feelings toward the person or situation?
8. **Journal Your Experience**: Write down any insights or feelings that came up during the meditation. What did you learn about yourself and your capacity to forgive?

Exercise 2: Gratitude and Resilience Reflection
Objective: To build resilience by focusing on gratitude, inspired by Corrie ten Boom's ability to find gratitude even in the darkest of times.
1. **Create a Gratitude Journal**: Begin a daily gratitude journal where you write down three things you are grateful for each day. These can be big or small things, such as "I am grateful for the sunshine today" or "I am grateful for the kindness of a friend."
2. **Reflect on Past Challenges**: Think about a challenging experience from your past that you were able to overcome. Reflect on the strengths, resources, or support that helped you through this time.
3. **Write a Letter of Gratitude to Yourself**: Write a letter to yourself expressing gratitude for the resilience and strength you showed during this challenging time. Acknowledge how this experience has helped you grow and what you learned from it.
4. **Identify Strengths Gained**: List 2–3 strengths or qualities you developed as a result of overcoming this challenge. For example, "I became more patient," or "I learned to trust myself more."
5. **Reflect on How These Strengths Can Help You Now**: Consider how these strengths can support you in your current life stage. How can they help you navigate new challenges or embrace new opportunities as you age?
6. **Share Your Gratitude**: If comfortable, share your gratitude reflections with a trusted friend or family member. Discuss how focusing on gratitude has impacted your mindset and resilience.

Corrie ten Boom provides practical ways for you to nurture your mind and spirit as you age. By focusing on vision, purpose, forgiveness, gratitude, and resilience, individuals can develop a growth mindset that empowers them to face life's challenges with grace and strength, ultimately finding joy and fulfillment at every stage.

Nelson Mandela's life: Lessons about purpose, leadership, and resilience.

Here are key takeaways from his journey:

1. **The Power of Forgiveness**: Despite spending 27 years in prison, Mandela chose reconciliation over revenge. His capacity to forgive those who oppressed him and his people highlights the strength of character it takes to build bridges rather than walls. This shows that true change comes through forgiveness, not retaliation.

2. **Perseverance in the Face of Adversity**: Mandela's long struggle against apartheid, including the hardship of imprisonment, teaches us the importance of perseverance. He endured unimaginable hardships, but he never gave up on his vision of a free and equal South Africa. This reminds us to stay committed to our goals, even when success seems distant or difficult.

3. **Purpose Sustains Us**: Mandela's life was driven by a deep sense of purpose—to end racial oppression in South Africa and establish a society based on justice and equality. His unyielding commitment to this purpose gave him the strength to endure isolation, hardship, and setbacks. It teaches us that a strong sense of purpose can carry us through even the darkest times.

4. **Leadership Through Example**: Mandela led by example, both in his activism and later as president of South Africa. He demonstrated humility, wisdom, and a willingness to serve others. His life shows that true leadership isn't about power or control, but about inspiring others and working for the greater good.

5. **Courage to Change**: Mandela's willingness to adapt and evolve in his thinking is also significant. Early in his life, he supported more militant tactics, but later, he embraced peace and reconciliation as the ultimate path to justice. His ability to change course when necessary, shows that wisdom often involves re-evaluating one's beliefs and strategies to achieve a higher purpose.

6. **A Vision Beyond Personal Gain**: Mandela's life was marked by selflessness. He didn't seek power for its own sake, but for the good of his country and its people. His story teaches us that living for something greater than ourselves—whether it's justice, equality, or love—brings the most enduring fulfillment.

7. **The Importance of Education and Knowledge**: Even during his imprisonment, Mandela understood the power of education. He encouraged others to learn and expand their minds, emphasizing that education is a critical tool for empowerment and freedom. His life reminds us that learning is essential for personal and societal transformation.

8. **Hope in Every Season of Life**: Mandela achieved many of his greatest accomplishments later in life, becoming president of South Africa at age 75. His story is a reminder that it's never too late to make a significant impact and that aging doesn't diminish our ability to lead and fulfill our purpose.

While studying Mandela's life, I learned that even in the face of overwhelming adversity, it's possible to stay true to a higher calling, act with compassion, and change the world for the better. Certainly!

Chapter 6, "**Focus on Purpose and Meaning**," will explore the importance of maintaining a sense of purpose and meaning in life, especially as one ages. As people grow older, their roles, responsibilities, and daily activities often change. Retirement, the loss of loved ones, or changes in physical health can lead to feelings of aimlessness or a loss of identity. However, finding new ways to cultivate purpose and meaning can lead to a more fulfilling and joyful life. Here is an expanded outline for Chapter 6:

By focusing on purpose and meaning, older adults can navigate the changes and challenges of aging with resilience and optimism. This chapter will provide practical advice, exercises, and inspirational stories to help readers embrace their later years as a time of growth, fulfillment, and joy.

Focusing on purpose and meaning as you age is essential for several reasons. It provides a foundation for emotional well-being, fosters a sense of belonging and significance, promotes mental and physical health, and helps individuals navigate the complexities and changes that come with aging. Here is a detailed exploration of the importance of maintaining focus and meaning as one ages:

1. Enhancing Emotional Well-being

- **Provides a Sense of Direction**: As people age, they often experience significant life changes, such as retirement, loss of loved ones, or changes in physical health. Having a clear sense of purpose and meaning can help provide direction and structure to daily life, offering a buffer against feelings of aimlessness or depression. ● **Boosts Self-Esteem and Confidence**: Engaging in meaningful activities that align with one's values and passions can boost self-esteem and confidence. This is especially important as traditional roles or identities, such as career or parenting, evolve or diminish in significance. Purpose-driven activities provide a sense of accomplishment and personal worth.

- **Reduces Risk of Depression and Anxiety**: Studies have shown that individuals who maintain a strong sense of purpose are less likely to experience depression and anxiety. Purpose provides a sense of control over one's life and can help mitigate the feelings of helplessness or hopelessness that sometimes accompany aging.

2. Promoting Mental and Cognitive Health

- **Keeps the Mind Engaged**: A sense of purpose often involves setting and pursuing goals, learning new skills, or engaging in meaningful activities—all of which keep the mind active and engaged. Mental stimulation is crucial for cognitive health and can help reduce the risk of cognitive decline and conditions such as dementia. ● **Encourages Lifelong Learning**: Purposeful aging often involves a commitment to lifelong learning and personal growth. This might include taking up new hobbies, attending educational courses, or engaging in creative pursuits. Lifelong learning fosters curiosity and mental agility, which are important for maintaining cognitive health.

- **Supports Resilience and Adaptability**: A strong sense of purpose can help older adults stay resilient in the face of challenges. When faced with adversity, such as health issues or the loss of loved ones, a clear sense of meaning can provide the motivation to adapt, persevere, and find new ways to live a fulfilling life.

3. Supporting Physical Health

- **Encourages Healthy Behaviors**: Individuals who have a strong sense of purpose are more likely to engage in healthy behaviors, such as regular exercise, a balanced diet, and adhering to medical advice. They are motivated to maintain their physical health so they can continue to pursue their passions and contribute to their communities.
- **Reduces Stress and Promotes Longevity**: A sense of purpose is linked to lower levels of stress and reduced risk of chronic diseases. Studies have shown that people with a strong sense of purpose tend to live longer and have better overall health outcomes. Purpose-driven living is associated with lower levels of inflammation and healthier cardiovascular profiles.
- **Facilitates Active Lifestyle**: A purposeful life often involves an active lifestyle. Whether through volunteering, community engagement, or physical activities like gardening or walking, staying active helps maintain physical fitness and mobility, which are crucial for aging well.

4. Fostering Social Connections and Belonging

- **Strengthens Relationships**: Having a sense of purpose often involves meaningful interactions with others. Whether it's through mentoring, volunteering, or participating in community or faith-based groups, these activities help build and maintain strong social connections. These connections are vital for emotional support, reducing feelings of loneliness, and fostering a sense of belonging. • **Encourages Intergenerational Relationships**: Purposeful living can encourage older adults to engage with younger generations, either through formal mentoring or casual interactions with family and community. These intergenerational relationships provide opportunities for sharing wisdom, learning from younger perspectives, and creating a mutually enriching environment.
- **Builds Community Engagement**: A strong sense of purpose can lead to active community involvement. Being part of a community, contributing to its growth, and fostering connections with others provides a sense of belonging and collective purpose. This engagement is often rewarding and reinforces the value of shared experiences and goals.

5. Providing Motivation and a Sense of Accomplishment

- **Drives Goal Setting and Achievement**: Purpose motivates individuals to set and pursue goals, which in turn fosters a sense of accomplishment and fulfillment. Even small achievements can provide satisfaction and reinforce the belief that life is meaningful and worthwhile.
- **Promotes a Positive Outlook on Aging**: A focus on purpose helps to reframe aging as an opportunity for growth, learning, and new experiences, rather than a period

- of decline. This positive outlook can reduce fear of aging and encourage a proactive approach to life's changes.
- **Encourages Resilience in Facing Life's Challenges**: Purpose provides a reason to continue moving forward, even when faced with life's inevitable challenges, such as health issues or the loss of loved ones. It helps older adults maintain a sense of agency and control over their lives.

6. Providing a Sense of Spiritual Fulfillment

- **Aligns with Spiritual or Religious Beliefs**: For many, a sense of purpose is deeply connected to spiritual or religious beliefs. Engaging in practices that align with these beliefs, such as prayer, meditation, or community service, can provide deep spiritual fulfillment and a sense of peace.
- **Offers Comfort and Hope**: Spiritual engagement and the search for deeper meaning often bring comfort, especially during difficult times. A strong spiritual foundation can offer hope, resilience, and a sense of connection to something greater than oneself.
- **Encourages Reflection and Legacy Building**: As people age, they often reflect on their life's journey and the legacy they wish to leave behind. Focusing on purpose and meaning can help guide this reflection, encouraging a life that aligns with one's values and desires to make a lasting impact.

7. Enabling Adaptation to Life's Changes

- **Facilitates Adjustment to New Roles**: As life circumstances change with age—such as transitioning from a career to retirement or becoming a caregiver—a sense of purpose helps individuals adjust to these new roles and find meaning in them. It encourages seeing these changes as opportunities for growth rather than losses.
- **Encourages Creative Problem-Solving**: Purpose-driven individuals are often more creative in finding solutions to new challenges. Whether it's finding new ways to stay active or engaging with others despite physical limitations, a strong sense of purpose fuels innovation and adaptability.
- **Helps Maintain Independence**: By focusing on activities and roles that bring meaning, older adults are more likely to maintain their independence and engage in self-care. Purposeful living often includes prioritizing one's well-being and finding ways to remain self-sufficient and empowered.

Focusing on purpose and meaning as one ages is more than just a philosophical pursuit—it is a vital aspect of healthy aging that impacts emotional, mental, physical, social, and spiritual well-being. By fostering a sense of purpose, older adults can navigate life's challenges with more vigor and clarity.

Ways to Embrace Joy and Gratitude

Power of Joy and Gratitude in Aging: Joy and gratitude are powerful tools for enhancing well-being. These positive emotions can help mitigate the challenges of aging, such as loneliness, grief, or health issues.

●

Benefits of Embracing Joy and Gratitude: There are physical, emotional, and social benefits of cultivating joy and gratitude, including reduced stress, improved relationships, better sleep, and increased overall life satisfaction.

1. Practicing Daily Gratitude

Keeping a Gratitude Journal: Writing down three to five things one is grateful for each day. This could be simple things like a warm cup of tea, a kind gesture from a friend, or a beautiful sunset. Journaling helps shift focus from what's lacking to what's abundant in life.

● **Gratitude Reflection**: Set aside a few minutes each day for a quiet moment of reflection, thinking about the positive aspects of life. Reflect on past experiences, relationships, and lessons learned, and recognize how these have shaped your life in meaningful ways.

● **Expressing Gratitude to Others**: Reach out to people who have made a difference in one's life. This could be through a handwritten note, a phone call, or a face-to-face conversation. Expressing gratitude strengthens relationships and fosters a deeper sense of connection.

2. Cultivating Joy in Daily Life

● **Mindfulness and Presence**: It is important to be fully present in each moment. Practicing mindfulness helps individuals savor the simple pleasures of life, like the taste of a meal, the sound of birds, or the warmth of the sun. Mindfulness practices can include deep breathing exercises, guided meditation, or mindful walking. ● **Engaging in Joyful Activities**: Engage in activities that bring you joy. This could include hobbies like gardening, painting, dancing, or playing a musical instrument. It is important to do what makes you happy and provides a sense of fulfillment. ● **Laughter and Playfulness**: Humor and playfulness are vitally important. Find ways to laugh daily, whether through watching a comedy, sharing jokes with friends, or playing games. Laughter can boost the immune system, reduce pain, and improve mood.

3. Nurturing Positive Relationships

● **Building and Maintaining Social Connections**: It is important to maintain and nurture relationships with family, friends, and community members. There are so many benefits of social engagement, such as reducing feelings of loneliness and enhancing feelings of joy and fulfillment.

● **Participating in Community and Group Activities**: Participate in community events, clubs, or faith-based activities. Being part of a group with shared interests can provide a sense of belonging and increase feelings of joy and connectedness.

● **Practicing Compassion and Kindness**: Small acts of kindness are a way to cultivate joy. This could be volunteering, helping a neighbor, or simply offering a smile or a kind word. Acts of kindness create a ripple effect of positivity and enhance both the giver's and receiver's sense of joy.

-   ●

4. Developing a Positive Mindset

-   ● **Reframing Negative Thoughts**: Identify and reframe negative thoughts. Encourage replacing negative self-talk with positive affirmations. For example, instead of thinking, "I'm too old to try new things," one could say, "I have a lifetime of experience to draw from as I try new things."
-   ● **Focusing on Strengths and Accomplishments**: Reflect on personal strengths and past achievements. Recognizing your capabilities and accomplishments fosters a sense of pride and joy, even in later years.
-   **Accepting and Embracing Change**: It is important to accept life's changes and transitions with grace. Adopting a mindset that sees aging as an opportunity for growth, wisdom, and new experiences, rather than a period of decline.

5. Spiritual Practices for Joy and Gratitude

-   ● **Incorporating Spirituality and Faith**: Engage in practices that bring peace and joy, such as prayer, meditation, or attending religious services. These practices can provide a sense of purpose, connection, and inner peace.
-   ● **Meditative Gratitude Practices**: Gratitude meditation practices focus on acknowledging and appreciating the good in life. This could involve visualizing a positive experience, expressing thanks to a higher power, or simply taking deep breaths while focusing on the feeling of gratitude.
-   ● **Creating a Gratitude Ritual**: Create daily or weekly rituals that focus on gratitude. This could be lighting a candle and offering thanks, creating a gratitude jar where one adds a note each day, or setting aside time for a family gratitude circle.

6. Engaging with Nature

-   ● **Nature Walks and Outdoor Activities**: Spending time outdoors, whether through walking, gardening, or simply sitting in a park. Being in nature has been shown to reduce stress, enhance mood, and foster a sense of wonder and joy.
-   ● **Mindful Observation of Nature**: Practice mindful observation by focusing on the sights, sounds, and smells of nature. This practice can bring a deep sense of peace and contentment and enhance the experience of the present moment.
-   ● **Bringing Nature Indoors**: If you have limited mobility, bring nature indoors, such as growing houseplants, creating a small indoor garden, or decorating with natural elements like stones, flowers, or shells.

7. Finding Joy in Small Moments

-   ● **Celebrating Small Wins**: Celebrate small achievements and milestones, no matter how minor they may seem. This could be cooking a favorite meal, completing a craft project, or even managing to get outside for a walk.
-   ● **Finding Joy in Routine Activities**: Find joy in everyday activities by being fully present and appreciating the moment. This could be savoring a cup of coffee, enjoying a good book, or listening to a favorite song.
-   ● **Practicing Gratitude for Everyday Blessings**: Look for blessings in everyday life. This could include appreciating good health, a loving family, a safe home, or the beauty

- of a sunrise. Recognizing these everyday blessings fosters a deeper sense of gratitude and joy.

8. Strategies for Sustaining Joy and Gratitude

- **Creating a Joy and Gratitude Routine**: Develop a daily or weekly routine that includes practices for joy and gratitude. This could be a morning gratitude journal, a weekly call with a friend, or a daily walk in the park.
- **Staying Positive Amidst Challenges**: Maintain joy and gratitude even during difficult times. This could include seeking support from loved ones, engaging in uplifting activities, or practicing acceptance and self-compassion.
- **Reflecting on Personal Growth and Gratitude**: Reflect on personal growth and the things one is grateful for. This can help reinforce a positive mindset and sustain feelings of joy and contentment over time.
- **The Lifelong Journey of Joy and Gratitude**: Summarize the key points discussed in this chapter and reinforce the idea that joy and gratitude are not just feelings but choices and practices that can be cultivated daily.
- **Encouragement to Embrace Joy and Gratitude:** Embracing joy and gratitude can lead to a more meaningful, fulfilled life, no matter one's age.

Conclusion: Embracing Aging with Purpose and Joy

Aging is an inevitable journey, but how we approach it can make all the difference. Throughout this book, we've explored various ways to embrace aging with grace, purpose, and joy. From nurturing the mind and spirit, maintaining physical wellness, cultivating meaningful relationships, and preparing for the future, each chapter has provided insights and strategies to help navigate the aging process with confidence and fulfillment.

Reflecting on the Journey

As we grow older, it's natural to encounter both joys and challenges. By adopting a growth mindset and remaining open to new experiences, we can continue to learn, adapt, and thrive. Embracing change, rather than fearing it, allows us to see aging as an opportunity for growth, reflection, and deeper self-understanding.

Fostering a sense of purpose and meaning is crucial at every stage of life. Whether through volunteer work, creative endeavors, or spiritual practices, finding ways to contribute to others and our communities enriches our lives and gives us a reason to look forward to each new day.

The Power of Gratitude and Joy

A key theme throughout this book is the power of gratitude and joy. By focusing on the positives and being thankful for the blessings we have, we cultivate a mindset that promotes happiness and well-being. Practicing gratitude daily, finding joy in small moments, and celebrating life's milestones—big or small—helps to maintain a positive outlook and fosters emotional resilience.

The Importance of Relationships

Our connections with others play a vital role in our well-being as we age. Whether through family, friends, or community, these relationships provide support, love, and a sense of

•

belonging. Nurturing these connections, even amidst the challenges of aging, is essential for emotional health and overall life satisfaction.

For those facing the complexities of caregiving, grief, or relationship changes, it's important to seek support and recognize that you're not alone. Building a strong support network and practicing effective communication can help navigate these transitions with compassion and understanding.

Taking Charge of the Future

Preparing for the future is an empowering process that allows us to take charge of our lives. Whether it's through financial planning, health care decisions, or creating a legacy, being proactive ensures that we are ready for the years ahead. It is never too early or too late to start thinking about the future. By taking steps now, we can reduce uncertainty and create a roadmap for a secure, fulfilled, and joyful later life.

A Call to Action: Aging with Intention

Aging with purpose and joy is not about denying the realities of getting older but about embracing this stage of life with intention, grace, and a positive spirit. It's about recognizing the wisdom that comes with age, honoring the journey we've traveled, and looking forward to the adventures that lie ahead.

Take this opportunity to reflect on the lessons and insights shared in this book. Consider the steps you can take today to enhance your well-being, build stronger relationships, and prepare for a meaningful future. Remember, aging is not just about adding years to life but adding life to years.

Final Thoughts

As you continue on your journey, may you find inspiration, peace, and joy in every step. Embrace the beauty of aging, cherish each moment, and live your life with purpose and gratitude. Aging is a privilege—a chance to experience the fullness of life, share wisdom, and leave a lasting impact on the world. Let's age gracefully, with open hearts, curious minds, and a spirit of joy.

Thank you for embarking on this journey with me. May your path be filled with light, love, and endless possibilities.

Foreword

This year I turned 65 years young and retired as senior pastor of the church I planted nearly 35 years ago. There were moments that I wondered if I was losing my strength and impact. But there were two things that helped me see differently. First, I began to look at all I had learned and how many people I could help. I realized that my age had put me in a place to share insight, encourage and help those younger avoid my mistakes. Secondly, I had the pleasure of coaching Shirley Breedlove. I got the chance to see first hand what Growing Older Gracefully looks like... and she made it beautiful!!
In this powerful Growing Older Gracefully, Shirley gives us the practical help that we need to get better than we have ever been before. Please read and write and grow. This is your time to shine and help those who still sit in darkness.

Courtney McBath
Business and Leadership Coach
Norfolk, Virginia

Courtney

Courtney McBath, DMin
ICF Certified Coach, ACC
Courtney McBath Coaching and Consulting, LLC

www.courtneymcbath.com

Shirley is a retired mental health counselor with over 40 years of dedicated service, helping individuals navigate their personal challenges and embrace their full potential. A proud graduate of Temple University, she holds both a Bachelor's and Master's degree in Social Work. In 2016, she earned certifications as a Health and Life Coach from the Health Coach Institute, and in 2022, she received her Certificate of Ministry from Healing the Soul Ministry.

Throughout her career, Shirley has remained committed to empowering individuals to fulfill their dreams. With extensive coaching experience, she has been blessed to learn from extraordinary mentors, including Dr. Courtney McBath, whose guidance encouraged her to dream bigger, and Rosalind Stanley, a long-time mentor and inspiration.

In addition to her coaching practice, Shirley recently relaunched her 501(c)(3) nonprofit organization to focus on supporting the homeless, veterans, individuals with mental illness, and those recovering from addiction. Through initiatives like a food pantry and youth mentoring programs, she is laying the groundwork for a *Dream Center*—a place dedicated to providing hope, resources, and mentorship for disadvantaged communities.

My Inspiration to write this book:

This book is a reflection of how I have lived my life, embracing the journey of aging with grace and purpose. My hope is to inspire young people to learn how to grow older gracefully *before* they reach their senior years. By adopting this mindset early, they can live with intention, build meaningful relationships, and find joy in every stage of life.

I believe deeply in the power of purpose and dreams to transform lives, and want to continue to inspire others to take bold steps toward achieving their goals.

Made in United States
Orlando, FL
30 March 2025

59990510R00024